Nikki Iles
Jazz on a Winter's Night

11 Christmas classics for jazz piano

MUSIC DEPARTMENT

OXFORD
UNIVERSITY PRESS

OXFORD
UNIVERSITY PRESS

Great Clarendon Street, Oxford OX2 6DP, England
198 Madison Avenue, New York, NY 10016, USA

Oxford University Press is a department of the University of Oxford.
It furthers the University's aim of excellence in research, scholarship,
and education by publishing worldwide

Oxford is a registered trade mark of Oxford University Press
in the UK and in certain other countries

ISBN 978-0-19-336590-2

Music origination by Barnes Music Engraving Ltd, East Sussex
Printed in Great Britain on acid-free paper by
Halstan & Co. Ltd, Amersham, Bucks

Credits

Cover illustration by Tony Stephenson © Oxford University Press
Artist photo by Hugh Byrne

The *Jazz on a Winter's Night* CD, featuring Nikki Iles, was recorded at
The Red Admiral studio by Steve Rose on 27 May 2009

Contents

Arranger's note

One of the most enjoyable aspects about working on this project has been seeking out tunes that lend themselves to a jazz treatment, and, to be honest, I was spoilt for choice.

It was always important to me that this collection should reflect the hybrid nature of jazz and demonstrate clearly how this music is more a process than a specific style. In many ways the hall-marks of a jazz performance are never fully notatable and so I have aimed instead for a series of atmospheres that will create the sensibility of an improvisation. In keeping with this ideal, I very much encourage users of this collection to expand upon the written material where they feel able to. Then, with any luck, these notated improvisations will prove to be a starting point for further seasonal creativity! Enjoy!

4

Have yourself a merry little Christmas

words and music
by HUGH MARTIN
and RALPH BLANE
arr. Nikki Iles

inspired by Nat King Cole

Winter Wonderland

words by DICK SMITH
music by FELIX BERNARD
arr. Nikki Iles

inspired by Take Six

I saw three ships

trad. English
arr. Nikki Iles

inspired by the Modern Jazz Quartet

In the bleak mid-winter

words by CHRISTINA ROSSETTI
music by GUSTAV HOLST
arr. Nikki Iles

inspired by Bill Evans

Noël nouvelet

trad. French
arr. Nikki Iles

inspired by the John Coltrane Quartet

Santa Claus is comin' to town

words by HAVEN GILLESPIE
music by J. FRED COOTS
arr. Nikki Iles

inspired by Paul Bley

The Christmas Song

('Merry Christmas to You')

words and music
by MEL TORMÉ
and ROBERT WELLS
arr. Nikki Iles

* Or:

inspired by Frank Sinatra

O little town of Bethlehem

trad. English
arr. Nikki Iles

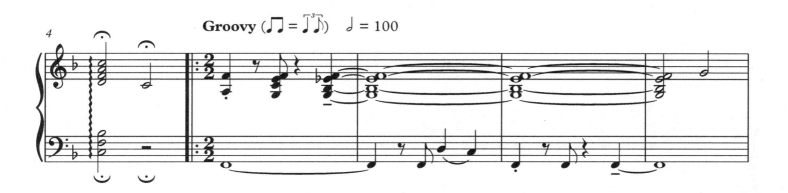

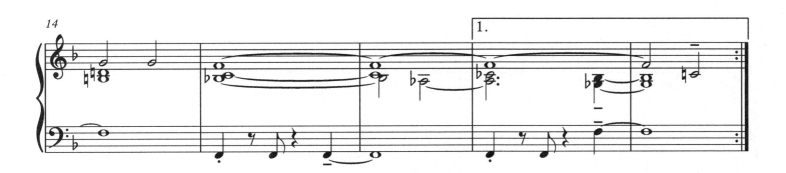

24

inspired by Vince Mendoza

Balulalow

words 16th century
music by PETER WARLOCK
arr. Nikki Iles

inspired by Norma Winstone

Sans Day carol

trad. English
arr. Nikki Iles

inspired by Abdullah Ibrahim

Silent night

orig. words by JOSEF MOHR
music by FRANZ XAVER GRUBER
arr. Nikki Iles

Very still ♩ = 80

inspired by Thad Jones